Discernment

A Path to Spiritual Awakening

Rose Mary Dougherty, SSND

Paulist Press
New York/Mahwah, NJ

Cover design by Joy Taylor

Book design by Sharyn Banks

Library of Congress Cataloging-in-Publication Data
Dougherty, Rose Mary, 1939–
    Discernment : a path to spiritual awakening / Rose Mary Dougherty.
        p. cm.
    Includes bibliographical references.
    ISBN 978-0-8091-4554-6 (alk. paper)
    1. Discernment (Christian theology) I. Title.
    BV4509.5.D66 2009
    248.4—dc22   2008047333

Published by Paulist Press
997 Macarthur Boulevard
Mahwah, New Jersey 07430

www.paulistpress.com
Printed and bound in the United States of America

Contents

Appreciations

I dedicate this work with affection and gratitude to Jerry Cambell, SJ, who first walked with me into the terrain of discernment, and to Charlotte Joko Beck and Janet Richardson, CSJP, Roshi, who opened me to new ways of seeing.

I also want to express my deep appreciation to colleagues and associates of Shalem Institute's Spiritual Guidance Program, whose receptive listening and probing questions brought me to a deeper level of my own experiential knowledge of discernment, as well as my appreciation to author Reynolds Price, who introduced me to Kate Vaiden, a fictitional but very real woman who learned early on, when she saw no precedent around her, to trust the deep guiding spirit within her. She continues to be an inspiration for me.

Finally I want to thank the many friends who have supported me in this writing, especially William Walsh, SJ; Bill Wyndaele, CICM; Mary Ann Buckley, SHCJ; and Monica Maxon and Clare Openshaw, who stayed with me through the final details.

Introduction

This book began in my heart many years ago when people encouraged me to share in writing my understanding of discernment. I felt that this outer encouragement was a confirmation of an inner calling I had been experiencing. I began my writing then and have returned to it faithfully each year. In a sense you might say I've been a perpetual servant of discernment. Sometimes there's been an urgency to "get it all right" for myself and others. At other times there has been just a simple appreciation of what is given when I put aside the urgency and reflect on my own experience in light of what I have read and heard from others.

For many years I had studied discernment and had tried to put into practice what I had learned in my daily living and decision making. There came a point, however, when I discovered that what I had learned didn't seem to illuminate what was going on in me. God seemed to be teaching me about discernment in a new way that had less to do with trying to apply what I had learned before and more to do with recognizing and trusting the discerning Spirit within me.

In retrospect, I realize that what I had learned, especially from Ignatian spirituality, had served me very well. My understanding offered signs and guideposts that were useful along the way, not just for me but for others as well, while at the same time making it very clear that no two people ever walked the exact same path of discernment. God's active presence within each of us is unique. We must listen deeply to that presence in all of life.

Yet it was difficult for me to live out the implications of this awareness, and it might be for you, too. It seemed much more comfortable and safe to rely on what I had learned theoretically and on the wisdom of other people than to act on what I had come to know experientially. I was too timid to trust my own experience; I was sure that others knew more about discernment than I did. Since then, it has become clear that discernment doesn't need to be an either/or—that is, something based either on my own experience or on that of others. But for a period of time, my reliance on others won out.

For many years, I had a recurring dream that illustrates this point. When I began to track the occurrences of this dream, I realized that invariably it showed up to announce some kind of transition, although I didn't always see that at the time. In the dream, I was trying to decide whether or not I should enter a religious community. I would go from one wisdom figure to the next, listening intently to each opinion of what I should do.

Several years ago, I had that dream again. However, something had changed. This time I approached the same wisdom figures as before, ready to elicit their advice, but I realized when I got to each one that I shouldn't ask my question. Finally I came to a beautiful little boy about five years old. He was the person it seemed I should ask and so I put my question to him, "Do you think I ought to be a sister?" He looked at me a long time and then responded simply, "Do you wanna?" Thus I began to encourage myself and others to listen to the "deep wannas" of our hearts.

When I started teaching discernment in the Spiritual Guidance Program of Shalem Institute for Spiritual Formation,[1] the essence of what I had learned began to unfold for me. I wanted to share that essence with others in a way that would make it their own: the theory of tradition might inform their experience, but God was truly at work in each human heart, leading each to *inner wisdom*. I wanted to facilitate people's sensitivity to the uniqueness of God's way of guiding them and their claiming of the ways they had come in touch with *wisdom* in their own lives. I wanted to assist their exploration of the gift of their experience as a vehicle for facilitating that knowing in others.

My students quickly became my teachers, as have all those I've accompanied in the process of spiritual direction and retreats. All of them have offered me new language and the gift of their experiences, thus broadening my understandings of discernment and assisting me in making the material more accessible to others. My own spiritual directors over the years have taught me much, especially through their patient insistence on my ongoing attention to God's guiding presence in the ordinary stuff of my life.

Writings other than those formally associated with discernment also brought new insights. The letters of the foundress of my religious community, the School Sisters of Notre Dame, opened the core of discernment for me in a very practical way. Mother Theresa Gerhardinger knew her own heart and the heart of the congregation she had founded. She nourished those hearts in prayer and constantly returned there in large decisions and small. She called us to do the same: "It is God who directs hearts like streams of water; to (God) let us pray."[2] Other particularly relevant writings were the works of Thomas Kelly and Douglas Steere, spiritual giants in the Quaker tradition, and Jean-Pierre de Caussade's *Sacrament of the Present Moment*.[3] Writings from the Zen tradition, especially those of Robert Kennedy, SJ, Roshi ("venerable teacher"), and Zen teacher Charlotte Joko Beck, have also given me new perspective.[4]

What I read of Joko Beck led me to believe that she could expand my understanding of discernment, even though we were coming from different traditions. Thus began a series of conversations with her and, soon after that, my practice of Zen meditation, first with Joko Beck as my teacher and then with Sister Janet Richardson, CSJP, Roshi. This practice continues to allow me to live with awareness in the present moment.[5]

Each of these sources of learning has enriched my understanding of discernment, thus informing what I choose to share with you now. I do not dismiss my early learnings about discernment, especially within the Ignatian framework. Those learnings have been pivotal to my writing but they are not the whole of it. They have proven to be a launch pad from which further reflection springs, not the termination point of my exploration.

The constant in my understanding and living of discernment is its integral relationship to prayer, for it is only through prayer that our lives are brought into focus and we begin to sense who we are and what we need to be about. I hope the interweaving of this theme throughout these reflections gives evidence of this conviction. There is no one definition, description, or practice of prayer that conveys the whole of it for me. I tend to relate prayer first of all to that abiding prayer in me, God's loving, God's yearning, God's prayer, and then to my intention to join that abiding prayer—the intention of freedom for love; the intention of compassionate action; the intention of living my true identity, abiding in love. Sometimes particular practices serve my intention. However, these are not the heart of prayer; they are only the means. As such, they change as I uncover new dimensions of intention. There are times when I realize that what I intend is, in fact, a reality. Then practices disappear completely, somewhat as the scaffolding of a building does when the building is completed. It doesn't mean that I will never return to those practices; it just means that they won't serve a purpose for a while. And, in fact, to hold on to a practice once it has outlived its purpose is to create an idol.

So if you were to ask me what prayer is, I would turn the question back to you: What is prayer for you? What honors your desire for God? What expresses the desire of your heart? Who are you? What allows you to live the fullness of your being? Allow your experience of prayer to be your guide as you move through these reflections.

A wise old friend of mine who was in his late eighties would often say to me, "Always something new to learn, isn't there, Rose Mary?" May we never have a self-contained, once-and-for-all understanding of discernment (or anything, for that matter). What I offer in these reflections is what I can see for now. I give them in the hope that my writing provides you an insight into what is real for you and offers you encouragement to continue your own exploration as you live more fully the wisdom of your being. May it be so!

1

An Overview
of Discernment

In my own reflection on and presentation of discernment, I find it important to consider some of the traditional understandings of the subject. It helps me get my moorings. Thus I offer this reflection as a road map for what will follow. However, you may find that you can appreciate the terrain without referring to this particular map. No matter what your familiarity with the topic of discernment, I would advise you, as I have said so often in the Shalem Institute's Spiritual Guidance Program, "Don't get bogged down by concepts or analysis. Let this initial material 'wash over you,' and see what, if anything, remains with you as you come to the end of this reflection."[1] It may well be that what you read here will only begin to make sense after you have spent time with the reflections that follow it.

Ignatius and Buddha

References to discernment appear throughout the history of Christian spirituality, and even before that, in writings about the life of the Buddha,[2] for example, although various writers may use different ways to name it. The literal translation of the word has its roots in the Greek *diakrisis*, which means "to separate," "to sift through," "to sort out," or "to distinguish." The following are examples of discernment from the lives of the Buddha and Saint Ignatius.

From the life of the Buddha we read:

> Before my self-awakening, when I was still just an unawakened Bodhisattva, the thought occurred to me: "Why don't I keep dividing my thinking into two classes?" So I made thinking imbued with sensuality, thinking imbued with ill will, and thinking imbued with harmfulness one class, and thinking imbued with renunciation, thinking imbued with non-ill will, and thinking imbued with harmlessness another class....And as I remained thus heedful, ardent, and resolute, thinking imbued with sensuality arose. I discerned that "Thinking imbued with sensuality has arisen in me; and that leads to my own affliction or to the affliction of others, or to the affliction of both. It obstructs discernment, promotes vexation, and does not lead to Unbinding."

And as I remained thus heedful, ardent, and resolute, thinking imbued with renunciation arose. I discerned that "Thinking imbued with renunciation has arisen in me; and that leads neither to my own affliction, nor to the affliction of others, nor to the affliction of both. It fosters discernment, promotes lack of vexation, and leads to Unbinding."[3]

From Saint Ignatius we read:

In reading the Life of our Lord and the lives of the Saints, he paused to think and reason with himself. "Suppose that I should do what St. Francis did, what St. Dominic did?" He thus let his thoughts run over many things that seemed good to him, always putting before himself things that were difficult and important which seemed to him easy to accomplish when he proposed them....These thoughts lasted a good while. And then other things taking their place, the worldly thoughts...came upon him and remained a long time with him. This succession of diverse thoughts was of long duration, and they were either of worldly achievements which he desired to accomplish or those of God which took hold of his imagination to such an extent, that worn out with struggle, he turned them all aside and gave his attention to other things.

There was however this difference. When he was thinking of things of the world he was filled with delight, but when afterwards he dismissed them from weariness, he was dry and dissatisfied. And when he thought of going barefoot to Jerusalem and of eating nothing but herbs and performing other rigors he saw that the saints had performed, he was consoled, not only when he entertained these thoughts, but even after dismissing them he remained cheerful and satisfied. But he paid no attention to this, nor did he stop to weigh the difference until one day his eyes were opened a little and he began to wonder at the difference and reflect on it, learning from experience that one kind of thoughts left him sad and the other cheerful. Thus, step by step, he came to recognize the difference between the two spirits that moved him....[4]

These examples from the lives of the Buddha and Ignatius illustrate what is meant by *diakrisis*, one of the skillful means needed to unlock the doors to a discerning heart. For some, however, this skillful means becomes the primary exercise of discernment; you may be aware of such skillful means operating in you. For example, you might notice that when you spend your time indulging in self-critical thoughts, you are also prone to negative thoughts toward others. You may realize that the fruit of such ideas is mostly negative pollution. On the other hand, when you are in a place of loving kindness toward yourself, not ignoring your mistakes and petty thoughts and actions but loving yourself through them, this kindness extends to others also.

Sometimes, as with anything, *diakrisis* can be carried to the extreme. We spend more time in the analysis of what has been than actually living in the moment. Perhaps it is easier and more tangibly rewarding to latch onto an analytical process that supports this "sorting out" than it is to cultivate a discerning heart, and yet a discerning heart is what discernment is really about. More often than not, material about discernment has encouraged a way of being or habit of the heart that disposes us to be responsive to God's discerning presence in our lives. The fruit of discernment is a deepening awareness of our oneness with all and a growing participation in God's caring love for all. Saint Ignatius speaks of this as "finding God in all things, in order that we might love and serve God in all."[5]

Discernment as Habit

Supporting the reflections in this book is the understanding that discernment is primarily a habit, a way of being that, while initially cultivated by our skillful means, ultimately takes us beyond them. Sometimes the habit of discernment invites specific acts, times of actively and consciously bringing particular decisions into prayer. These acts of discernment may include "sorting through" experiences and information related to the decision so that we might see freshly in the moment and choose that which best fits our being. But, decision making is only one facet of discernment. It can, in fact, be the need to make a decision that becomes the catalyst for the cultivation of a discerning heart that serves us in all of life.

Sometimes people will show up for spiritual direction saying, "I need you to help me make an important decision." When I ask how they have prayed about the decision, I often find they haven't at all. They've thought a lot about their decision and scrutinized their lives in relation to it, but there's been no prayer, no intentional being with God in the process. Thus they've been constrained by their habitual ways of seeing. There has been no space for the new. So I encourage them to begin where they are, to pray as they can in this moment, with this decision. More often than not, this time of prayer becomes the foundation for an ongoing life of prayer and a conscious choice to live differently, to see with new eyes.

This discernment that I speak of is a gift that has been given all of us. We don't create it; we don't receive it from someone. Perhaps we might say that we uncover it and nourish it. We uncover the gift and then we nourish it through the skillful means of noticing, through our prayer, and through our growing openness to God in all of life. We sensitize ourselves to the uniqueness of discernment through ongoing attentiveness to our experience in prayer and reflection and often through the assistance of spiritual direction and companionship, wherein others pray with and for us and offer us the glimmers of what they see in our story to help us recognize what we might not see alone. We might also clarify our understanding through listening to the experience of others and reading some of the classical literature on discernment. The danger in any of this is that we begin to view others as experts who possess a special power that we don't have. But their advice is, in most cases, a distillation of personal experiences informed by tradition. They are therefore no more or less gifted in discernment than we are. They are simply gifted in *assimilating their experience* and making it available to us; for this we thank God.

Saint Ignatius of Loyola is one such person. He was a student in the school of prayer as taught through life experience before he ever made his learning available to others. This is what makes his writing, especially as presented in his *Spiritual Exercises*, so relevant for us. The *Spiritual Exercises* flow from the prayer and the experiential learning of the saint, and they reflect much of the classical understandings of discernment in his day. They were meant to be used within the context of a retreat, which could assist others in claiming their unique experience of God and help them respond authentically to God's presence in their lives. Thus the *Spiritual Exercises* were meant to foster the habit of discernment, a discerning way of life. Without the experience of the retreat, a person might miss the primary intent of the *Spiritual Exercises* and get caught in the methods presented in them.

At the heart of Saint Ignatius's writings was the openness to listening deeply to the spirit within. He told the people who would direct others in Ignatian spirituality to "listen deeply with the person." His description of the spiritual director in the *Spiritual Exercises* suggests an image of that person as a good maître d' who perceives when each course is ready and serves it graciously and thoughtfully to his guests. He reminds the director "that God is not only Creator but truly the Director."[6]

It took me a while to understand this concept. It wasn't until I had completed a thirty-day Ignatian retreat during which I constantly pestered my director for answers, and then had directed several people myself, that I finally understood what Saint Ignatius was suggesting. I don't think I did much harm in those early days. I suspect coordinators for those retreats assigned to me well-seasoned people who knew what they were about in the retreat and could tolerate a "rookie." These retreatants taught me and drew me into their prayer.

It goes without saying that the insights Saint Ignatius offered in the sixteenth century continue to make an invaluable contribution to the understanding of discernment today. What follows is a brief look at some of the key concepts in Ignatian spirituality; subsequent reflections will present themes related to discernment.

Saint Ignatius's best-known work, *The Spiritual Exercises*, might better be called *A School of Discernment*. Some critics of his approach suggest that it encourages us to move out of a place of prayer into a place of analysis and self-scrutiny. However, at the very beginning of the *Exercises* the retreatant is reminded, "In the spiritual exercises which follow, we find ourselves sometimes doing much thinking and reasoning things out. At other times, we experience far more the response of our hearts, with little or nothing for the head to be concerned about. It is good to remember that we are always in the context of prayer, whether meditative or affective, and so we should always try to maintain a spirit of deep reverence before God."[7] The *Anima Christi* (Soul of Christ) prayer that introduces the text of the *Exercises* gets to the heart of what they are about:

> Jesus, may all that is you flow into me.
>
> May your body and blood be my food and drink.
> May your passion and death be my strength and
>   life.
> Jesus, with you by my side enough has been given.
> May the shelter I seek be the shadow of your cross.
> Let me not run from the love that you offer,
> But hold me safe from the forces of evil.
> On each of my dyings shed your light and love.
> Keep calling me until that day comes,
> When, with all your saints, I may praise you
>   forever. Amen.[8]

Discernment of Spirits and Discernment of God's Will

In the *Spiritual Exercises*, Saint Ignatius describes two facets of discernment: the discernment of spirits and the discernment of God's will. Both of these may be viewed as different forms of the *diakrisis* spoken of earlier. Although there are many references to both of these facets of discernment throughout the literature of Christian spirituality, it seems only fair to acknowledge that there are differing interpretations and approaches to the concepts. What I present here is my understanding of the perspective Saint Ignatius offered.

Discernment of spirits is concerned with the discrimination of interior movements, those attractions or nudgings of the heart that evoke a response or move us toward a particular action. This discrimination involves observing those interior movements that ignite the flame of our desire for God and encourage our own authenticity, and those that appear to direct our attention and aspiration away from God and our true selves. The purpose of this discrimination would be to facilitate a growing self-knowledge that frees us to move in harmony with those movements that draw us toward God. Such discrimination could also provide the alertness we need to avoid being swept away by those interior nudges that move us away from God and from our true selves, as seen in the examples from the lives of the Buddha and Saint Ignatius cited earlier. Both became sensitized to the patterns of thoughts that held them captive and to those that freed them.

The key to our discrimination is simple awareness of inner stirrings without analysis. At best, we can say these stirrings "seem to be leading to, or inviting." Generally only with a great deal of hindsight can we know where something has been leading. For this reason, the *Spiritual*

Exercises suggest that we "track" a movement from the beginning, through the middle, to the end to see where it might be leading. We may never be sure of the origin of the nudge, but we can notice its direction, watching it for a while before we allow it to inform decisions. Sometimes this is difficult to do, we want to run ahead of what we are being given. Each of us can probably recognize times in our lives when this has happened. For me, it occurs most subtly but forcefully when I am attached to a need for solutions or outcomes. Perhaps this example from my own life will help put you in touch with the way this happens for you in your life.

During a time of transition in my own life, I began to notice in myself a stirring of confidence that seemed very much like a gift, a grace. There was no particular object for this confidence—just a deep trust in God's abiding Spirit and my essential goodness. For a while I was able to just appreciate it, letting it animate my life. Then I began to notice a shift. Having grown tired of waiting for direction in my life, I had moved from being in the present moment to a future moment and thus seeking a future meaning. In doing so, I got separated from the stirring of confidence and its origin and was beginning to act precipitously out of its energy. What had been given as grace for the present was being used to secure the future. I had moved from a stance of listening to an old mode of "responsibly figuring out." In classical discernment terms you might say that I had stopped being open to "discerning God's will."

Discerning of God's will is concerned with recognizing and making choices congruent with who we are in God. We often recognize those choices as those which seem to offer life for ourselves and others and thus are probably "more conducive to the glory of God," the God whose glory is our being fully alive, as Irenaeus reminded us.

The matter of discerning the will of God has probably claimed more attention than any other facet of discernment. Unfortunately, much of the literature has been distilled into processes to help us "get it right," ignoring the core of discernment, that we "pray that God enlighten and move (us)."[9] I suspect this is so because we share a common desire to want to live authentically, and many of us equate that with getting all our decisions right. The literature and methods vary because, while many people speak of discerning the will of God, there are differing views on how the will of God is manifest in our lives. Some people reject the notion of God's will entirely and yet are able to pray to be aware of God's unique invitations to them. Others might have strong reservations about God having any particular will for them at all, while still others see God's will as extending to every facet of their lives. Some people believe that God doesn't care about the little decisions, just the big ones, so they begin to make artificial distinctions between what they bring to prayer and what they exclude. Others see God's will as something totally apart from them, something that God even hides from them until they are able to find the right clues, usually looking outside themselves, to discover it. Some see God's will as being embedded in themselves.

Often what we believe and what we know from our experience of God's will is not reflected in how we go about making decisions. For instance, I am one of those people who see God's will as fully embedded in who I am. Yet, in the example from my life that I cited previously, I had lost touch with what I truly believed and had stepped outside myself to look for direction. I do not mean to imply here that I would never look outside myself. I need to read the "signs" outside me, but I do so from the perspective of my inner core.

A crucial role of the literature on the discernment of God's will is, I think, the encouragement to reflect on our own experience and then seek to live in the authenticity of who we are. No method can give us this. It can, at best, clear away the debris of our hearts so we can enter unencumbered into prayer.

Consolation and Desolation

Before leaving this introductory material, it seems wise to consider two other key concepts that find their way into many conversations about discernment and the spiritual life in general: consolation and desolation.

There are few concepts in the language of spirituality subject to such diverse interpretations as these, not only among different schools of spirituality but also within the same school.[10] These differing interpretations can serve to remind us to look beneath language to the reality being expressed and, even once we are aware of the reality, to be slow to draw conclusions that suggest a particular course of action.

It is difficult to discuss spiritual consolation and desolation separately. As with other contrary experiences in the spiritual life, we may best describe or define one in terms of a lack of the other.

In referring to spiritual consolation in his writings on discernment, Saint Ignatius employs phrases such as "being aflame with intense love of God," "pouring out tears moving to love of God," and "finding our life of faith, hope, and love so strengthened and emboldened that the joy of serving God is foremost in our life." He encourages us to receive with gratitude the gift that has been given and to savor it.

Saint Ignatius describes desolation as everything that is contrary to spiritual consolation. He uses phrases such as "confusion," "gloom," "disquiet from various temptations and commotions," "difficulty in and distaste for prayer," "movement to contemptible and earthly things" and "tending toward lack of faith, hope, or love."[11]

Some interpreters of Saint Ignatius define consolation and desolation in terms of the direction of the movement of the heart, being drawn toward or away from God; they attach little or no importance to the felt experiences that accompany such movement. For instance, one could be in great pain at the prospect of the letting go required in a particular choice while still being very drawn to God in that decision. That has certainly been true for me in various decisions of my life, especially in my decision to leave the place of work I truly loved, Shalem Institute. I sensed the rightness of the decision but there was also much sadness connected with it and even some apprehension about what might be next in my life. Contradictory feelings also have surfaced in some seasons of my life when there has been great joy as I have lived into new freedom mixed with sadness at having to let go of behaviors or images of myself that didn't fit with that freedom.

In keeping with this understanding of consolation, John of the Cross[12] speaks of an increase of an esteeming love of God that values God above all else and draws the heart into a love that has little to do with felt passion or even joy. In John's understanding, it is precisely this love that evokes sadness and concern over what feels like a decline of faith, hope, or love. For John, this decline may have to do very much with God's purifying spirit detaching us from images of ourselves or God related to faith, hope, and love, rather than being the work of an undermining spirit.[13]

In considering consolation and desolation, it seems important not to allow our awareness of their presence or absence to become the basis of our judgment of what is going on between ourselves and God (as though we could really know anyway). We might be feeling distanced from God and equate that with God moving away from us. Or we may be experiencing a real distaste for prayer, which in turn makes us sad because we truly do want God to be the center of our lives. What may be more important than the awareness of consolation and desolation is the awareness of our desire for God, or our desire to desire God, underneath whatever it is we are experiencing. At such times we must trust that God does desire us.

One scholar of Ignatian spirituality says of discernment of spirits in consolation and desolation: "Desire is the key to discernment. It is a more reliable criterion than feelings or inner peace....Our habitual inner peace may be lacking, yet we still 'hang on' to the desire to love and serve....The desire to love arising within us is the basic criterion for recognizing the transformation of our inner experience by the Holy Spirit."[14]

Often it is precisely our desire to love that makes discernment difficult. The real pain and sadness in the experience of desolation is that we fear we are losing our fervor, our love for God, and our compassion for others. Here, especially, the praying, listening, and companioning of another in spiritual direction can be extremely helpful. Spiritual directors can help us hear, through the description of our experience and our concern about it, what our real desire is. They can help us claim what we really want.

There can also be pain and confusion in the felt experience of joyful attraction to God, or the ease of prayer. We can wonder if we are being deluded, if we really are praying. This concern can subtly shift our focus from God to ourselves. Once again, spiritual directors can help us look beneath our concern to our desire to be open to God, which is the heart of prayer.

Saint Teresa of Avila and Saint Ignatius offered assistance for discernment that can help shed light on our lived experience. In doing so, they use the language of "good spirit" and "evil spirit." I prefer to use the terms "friend of my authentic self" and "enemy of my authentic self." I explore these concepts with examples in other reflections, but it seems important to include them here. Both ideas suggest, although in different language, the following guidelines:

- For the person desiring God, the friend of our authentic self is usually one of gentleness and peace while the enemy of our best self is noisy and sometimes violent.

- The enemy of our authentic self often acts in secret, encouraging us not to speak of our confusion. It is often dispelled by our willingness to disclose our confusion to another. (Saint Teresa of Avila insisted on spiritual direction for her sisters.)

- The enemy of our authentic self often plays on our weakness. The antidote for this deception is prayer for self-knowledge and trust in God.

- The enemy of our authentic self may seek to dissuade us from our good purposes and from becoming who we really are by telling us it's too much for us, that we will lose too much, or that we can't possibly do it. The friend of our authentic self encourages us to a resoluteness, to continue to act out of our authentic desires.

Finally, both Saint Teresa and Saint Ignatius remind us that sometimes the experience of desolation is meant for our good, to allow us to see through to our desire for God that can be constant, despite what we are feeling. The experience of desolation can also draw us into a greater reliance on God rather than on what we can do for God.[15]

Spiritual consolation and desolation may be *experiences* of our relationship with God or they may offer *insight* into what's going on in our relationship with God, but they are not, in and of themselves, our relationship with God. It is easy, however, to give them too much attention or to misread what they have to tell us about our relationship with God. This latter point is well illustrated by a story Evelyn Underhill tells of a woman who thanked her profusely for the books she had written. The woman said to her: "I do so want to tell you that I always keep your dear books on a table by my bed; and I don't know whether it is your dear books, or whether it is my soft white bed, but directly I lie down and I do have the most wonderful illuminations from the Absolute."[16]

It can be tempting to covet the experience this woman describes or to do our best to avoid any experience of "dis-ease" in our spiritual life. Yet Jean-Pierre de Caussade, author of the spiritual classic, *The Sacrament of the Present Moment*, goes so far as to say that God "wishes to arouse anxiety and mistrust in us so that we should totally depend on [God.]"[17] There is the need then to return periodically to that classic discernment question, "What do I want: the consolation of God or the God of consolation?" and to Teresa of Avila's caution against praying for experiences of consolation lest we begin to try to create these experiences.[18] Finally, when we find ourselves caught in the analysis and judgment of our experiences of consolation and desolation, we may do well to listen freshly to the reminder of John of the Cross to pay less attention to our experience of God and more attention to the fruit of the experience.[19]

Listening to the Many Voices of God

What Saint Ignatius and others would consider the fruit of a discerning life I would also consider the grounding for such a life, the habit of discernment. In my view, an understanding of the habit of discernment is intrinsic to our understanding of the various concepts we consider in relation to discernment. It is the heart of discernment, and I will return to it often in these reflections.

The habit of discernment is an attitude of listening to God in all of life. It is, in the words of Saint Benedict, listening "with the ear of the heart."[20] It is a life of prayerful attention to God—a contemplative stance that Thomas Kelly refers to as "simplification" and that he describes as living "with a singleness of eye, from a holy Center where…we are wholly yielded to God."[21] As we seek to live in that holy Center we come to know who we are in God, we become who we truly are, and we are at home in God. In that place of at-homeness we seek to sensitize our hearts to God's presence in our lives. The eye of the heart grows accustomed to recognizing, almost spontaneously, those movements that are drawing us into oneness with ourselves and all creation in God and those that tend to isolate us even from ourselves.

Inherent in this discussion on the habit of discernment is the belief that God is actively and caringly involved with us in every moment of our lives, even the seemingly most mundane ones. Not only is God present with us, God's Spirit, Inner Wisdom, guides us to authentic expression of God's presence with us in each moment. We become who we truly are as we live in congruence with Inner Wisdom. For our part then, according to de Caussade: "All that is necessary is to love and accept the present moment as the best, with perfect trust in God's universal goodness."[22] Not only do we want to love in each present moment, we want to become aware of God's presence with us in each of our moments. We want to be attuned to Inner Wisdom guiding us toward love moment by moment.

The habit of discernment fine-tunes the ear of the heart so that we hear more clearly the invitations to love intrinsic to every moment of life. In the habit of discernment, our choices are again and again refined by the invitations to love. Gradually we come to know what is consonant with love, what we need to do or need not to do and, with grace, we are free to respond.

As stated in the beginning of this reflection, discernment is a gift that has been given all of us. We may become separated from it, lose sight of it, stop believing in it, but it is there waiting for us. Perhaps we need to pray that the eyes of our hearts be opened so we can see the gift that is there and look to the practices and people that might encourage us to cultivate our discerning hearts.

2

Openness to God

The habit of discernment is an attitude of listening to God in all of life. We might also describe it as a posture of openness to God in all of life or simply as prayerfulness. Some would name it active awareness. Others would talk about living fully out of our Sacred Source.

However we name it, it is important to reiterate that the habit of discernment is a gift. It is a gift that we may cultivate by praying intentionally and specifically in whatever way is right for us to be grounded in this habit. Our prayer begins, I think, as we say as wholeheartedly as possible: "This is what I want. This is how I want to live." We might ask to remember our desire for God all through the day. We may ask to see ourselves and others with God's eyes. Or we may simply be present in an attitude of openness to God in wordless prayer, allowing God's prayer in us to fill our hearts and overflow in compassion for our world.

Intentional Prayer

Our prayerfulness is also nourished by times that we set aside on a regular basis just to be with God. Because this prayer is really an expression of our awareness of God's presence with us, its form and content will be shaped by our sense of that presence. Both form and content will change as does our awareness. The prayer will reflect something of who we sense ourselves to be in God and who God is for us. As we move from the duality of two to the unity of one—"It is no longer I who live, but it is Christ who lives in me" (Gal 2:20)—our prayer becomes one of simple, active, loving presence. We are the living prayer of Jesus, "may all be one" (John 17:21).

Contemplative Practices

Contemplative practices that sharpen our awareness of reality also nourish the habit of discernment. These practices can open us to the dismantling of the clutter that covers our discerning hearts. They can bring us to our Center where we live more fully in the present moment so that in any given moment we can see what there is to see and respond freshly from who we are in this moment.

Rachel Naomi Remen, storyteller and early pioneer of mind/body health, describes what living in the Center might look like:

> In bullfighting there is a place in the ring where the bull feels safe. If he can reach this

place, he stops running and gathers his full strength. He is no longer afraid....It is the job of the matador to know where this sanctuary lies, to be sure the bull does not have time to occupy his place of wholeness.

This safe place for a bull is called the *querencia*. For humans the querencia is the safe place in our inner world....When a person finds their querencia, in full view of the matador, they are calm and peaceful. Wise. They have gathered their strength around them.[1]

Contemplative practices involve coming to our querencia, our Center, and once there, simply being present to what is, allowing ourselves to observe what is without the need to alter it. We might notice things like our breathing or an emotion, or something outside ourselves like a shadow on a wall. We see, without thinking about or defining what we see. Gradually the distinctions between ourselves and what we see disappear. We are in oneness with God.

Contemplative practices also include allowing built-in reminders in our lives, such as the ringing of the phone, the crying or laughter of a child, or the picture we see when we enter our office, to invite us back to the present moment so we can live intentionally where we are. We might couple such practices with a prayer like that of the Sioux Native Americans, which asks the Great Spirit to "enlighten our hearts" so that we might "see everything"

and through this vision help our neighbor.[2] We may look
to the prayer from the Book of Wisdom:

> That she may send (wisdom) forth from your
> holy heavens...that she may labor at my side,
> and that I may learn what is pleasing to you. For
> she knows and understands all things, and she
> will guide me wisely in my actions. (Wis 9:10–11)

More simply, we might pray to remember God and our
desire for God.[3]

Prayerful Reflection on One's Day

One contemplative practice long associated with discernment is the practice of prayerfully reflecting on our
day, traditionally called "the examen of consciousness."
In this practice, we want to be aware of the unique ways
God has been present for us during the past twenty-four
hours, the unique invitations to love that have been present during that time and how we have missed, responded
to, or resisted those invitations. Such awareness can lead
to a growing sensitivity to God in the very midst of our
busyness. So we pause for ten or fifteen minutes, usually
at the same time each day, asking God to narrate for us
the events and encounters of the past twenty-four hours.
We look with God at these events and encounters from
the vantage point of the present moment, somewhat as the
Buddha and Saint Ignatius did when they recalled their

thoughts. We allow our hearts to rest in whatever prayer might be there for us as we see God's perspective on our life, as we see our life from the Center. Ending this time of prayer, we might look ahead to the day that is coming—people we will be with, jobs to be done, and so on. We might notice the emotions that well up within us as we visualize the day, or how we are feeling pulled from our Center in what we see. We might once again claim our desire to live the coming day in the freedom of love. This prayer is not an attempt to master the day but rather our way of acknowledging how we want to live. As we are able to view the past in the present moment more freely and without attachment or judgment, it gradually becomes possible for us to stand in each present moment unencumbered and respond to what is given us.

Often, in the very act of praying over events that are to come, we begin to see more clearly "the tactics of the matador" within us that keep us from living in our querencia. Our growing familiarity with these tactics can release us from their hold and free us for compassionate action. Little by little we come to live more habitually in our querencia.

I have noticed another benefit to this practice. After I have utilized it for a while, I am less apt to see my life as a series of fragmented events and more apt to see it as the seamless garment that it really is. This somehow clarifies my discernment of choices. It makes it simpler to see what fits and doesn't fit with who I am.

Spiritual Direction

Another useful practice for those seeking to cultivate a discerning life is that of spiritual direction, also called spiritual guidance, spiritual companioning, or spiritual friendship. The Buddha called it "friendship with admirable people."[4] Whatever the name, it is an ongoing practice of meeting with another person or group in an environment of attention and intention, specifically for the purpose of heightening our sensitivity to who we are, how the God-life reveals itself in us and in all of life, how our choices and our responses reflect our being-in-God, and the tactics of the matador that tend to move us from our Center. Spiritual direction is never a substitute for our prayer and our ongoing attentiveness to God. Rather it is meant to support us in that which we most want. Today there are many different schools of thought on spiritual direction. I will elaborate on my view of it later in my reflections.

For centuries, faithful people have been concerned about discernment. Permeating the concern has been a yearning to live authentically with God and a desire to have that yearning penetrate and inform all of life. Sometimes it seems this very yearning moves us away from living our being with God into a mode of figuring out how to be with God. When that happens, discernment becomes a goal rather than the living process that is our life with God.

In cultivating the habit of discernment, we are invited to let go of the goal, to allow our lives "to flow unceasingly in that deep unknown where all that is neces-sary is to love and accept the present moment as the best, with perfect trust in God's universal goodness."[5] For truly "if anyone is seeking God, the Beloved is seeking that person much more."[6] The habit of discernment is about coming to live in the oneness of God's desire and ours. Finally, it is about an unrestricted love in all of life.

3

Freedom for Love

Discernment is ultimately about love. It is about see-ing, in the moment, the loving action and compassionate action that is mine and having the freedom to respond and to act. The freedom I am speaking of is an interior freedom. It is often described as an attitude of total recep-tivity to God.

Julian of Norwich describes free persons as those who are "so attached to God that there can be no created thing between (their) God and (themselves)."[1] We recog-nize this freedom in moments in which our desire for God is greater than our desire for anything else. This freedom is at the heart of who we are. It is not something we acquire; it is something we live into. As we come to live more and more in that place of true identity, we are grasped by Love. Pedro Arrupe, former Superior General of the Society of Jesus, speaks of this as "finding God, that is, then falling in love in a quite absolute, final way."[2] That love gradually determines all our choices. We begin to awaken to the invitations issued by love and are ready to respond out of the authenticity of our being.

Freedom and Unfreedom

If this freedom is our true essence, why is it that it seems so seldom available to us? Most of us have a history of being separated from ourselves. With good reason Paul admonishes us, "Do not be conformed to this world" (Rom 12:2). I would identify the world as aspects of our culture, our personal histories, our self-expectations, and all influences that contribute to the formation of a false identity. We get glimpses of what this false identity might be when we observe our "unfreedoms," what we cling to in place of love. Nothing need separate us from the love of God, but in fact, things do, because we try to make them God, we make the means an end. Often our attachments delude us into believing we are going for love when, in fact, we are settling for much less.

We get glimpses of our true identity as we claim the places of freedom in our lives, the times we've opted for love despite the risk. Sometimes our opting for love may seem very small and inconsequential in our eyes, but it is a choice to live into the freedom we have in the moment. We may not look like Francis of Assisi, Etty Hillesum, Martin Luther King Jr. or Mother Teresa, but we are living who we are. We need to be aware of the freedom that is ours.

This awareness of our freedom, or lack thereof, is not given to us in a vacuum. More often than not, it is given us in the context of life itself. Sometimes it is in our prayer around specific decisions that we see areas of unfreedom, the nonnegotiables of our heart that limit our freedom to choose. We can't make ourselves free at those times, but we can pray that at least in the particular decision we are making we don't choose from the place of unfreedom.

At times we may need to acknowledge that we don't even want to consider the possibility of freedom in a particular choice. We may recognize that we are "hooked" in a particular way and prefer to stay that way. This acknowledgement of our unfree self to God may be our greatest act of trust. A prayer in this place might sound like, "God, this is where I am right now. I wish I could choose from a different place, but I'm not there yet. Maybe some day I will be, but for now, I just trust that you are with me as I move ahead from the place where I am."

As stated earlier, discernment doesn't only have relevance for times of decision making. It is a stance, a way of being in all of life. That is why all of life can also teach us much about our unfreedom. For instance, we might be at a meeting and find ourselves turning off the person in the room who may have the most to tell us simply because we don't like the person. Or we might find ourselves resisting an inclination for a particular spiritual practice even though the inclination does not go away. Or we might refuse an invitation to a new way of being in a given circumstance just because we've come to identify ourselves with a particular role and don't want to give it up.

Often we choose to ignore emerging freedom because it is easier to do that than to risk the change that might accompany that freedom. Sometimes we may not recognize our freedom until love catches us off guard and evokes a freedom we didn't know we had. I remember a woman telling me about her addiction to smoking. It got so bad that this addiction began to dictate most of her decisions—whom she would spend her time with, where she would travel, and so on. Then her sister became very ill and was dying in a hospital. The woman wanted to be with her sister every minute but she constantly found herself leaving the room and spending a lot of time getting to a place where she could smoke. Finally she said to herself, "That's enough; this smoking is taking me away from what I most want." And she quit.

Then there is the story of Dr. Annalena Tonelli, who has dedicated her life to the health of the people of Somalia. She is quoted as saying, "I am desperately in love with TB patients....I want to be poor up to the last day of my life....I would never be able to render service if I had clothes and furniture and all the things which are normal for our society."[3]

These are seemingly very different examples with very different consequences. The point is, however, that love, a very particular love in a concrete circumstance, evoked a specific face of freedom for each of these women.

Samyutta Nikaya describes the process of unfolding freedom we see in the lives of these two women:

You should roam in places that are your own, that arise in accordance with your own true nature. And what is the place that is your own? It's the pasture of ardent clearness and mindfulness, where discontent and greed are put aside for the sake of the world. That is your own place, your natural range.[4]

Self-Knowledge and Interior Freedom

How is it that we come to live in our "own place," to abide in love, and to be love? For our part, I think, we open ourselves to seeing ourselves just as we are. We seek to know the truth of who we are so the truth may set us free (cf. John 8:32). In other words, we seek self-knowledge.

Spiritual giants of most religious traditions speak of the need for self-knowledge. Some see it as a prerequisite for interior freedom. I would say that it is a companion to interior freedom. This self-knowledge is not meant for our own programs of self-mastery. It's not meant to be the vehicle through which we make ourselves acceptable for ourselves and others. Anthony de Mello reminds us, "The fact of the matter is that you're neither OK nor not OK. You may fit the current mood or trend or fashion! Does that mean that you've become OK? Does your OK-ness depend on that? Does it depend on what people think of you? Jesus Christ must have been pretty not OK by those standards. You're not OK and you're not not OK, you're you."[5] It is our willingness to accept ourselves as okay or not that frees us to see ourselves as we are.

There may come a time for the pruning of our attachments, yet as Thomas Kelly tells us, "Prune and trim we must, but not with ruthless haste and ready pruning knife, until we have reflected upon the tree we trim, the environment it lives in, and the sap of life which feeds it."[6] Kelly is inviting us to self-knowledge, the growing awareness of who we truly are—who we are in God. We seek this knowledge so we can live discerning lives, living more fully who we are, and making choices congruent with our true identity. Such knowledge expands us, giving us our place in the universe story, freeing our hearts for compassion. Patricia Mische of Global Education Associates, an international network of individuals and organizations dedicated to global interdependence, reminds us of this when she says:

> Paradoxically the more deeply inward we go and the more we live in deep awareness of our own sacred center and source, the more universal we become; the more we grow in awareness of our deep unity with all peoples. The joys and sufferings of the world's peoples are our joys and sufferings. We are part of one humanity. The struggles and hopes of the world's people are our struggles and hopes. Their loss is our loss. Their discovery and growth is our discovery and growth.[7]

Such self-knowledge can only be the fruit of prayer; it is not the product of programs of self-scrutiny or self-improvement, or even tools like the Enneagram, Myers-Briggs, or other programs of self-discovery. Any of these, if used lightly and reverently, can give us tiny insights into ourselves and our way of relating to ourselves and the world so long as we are willing to test this learning in the crucible of prayer. Too often, however, we tend to cling to what they tell us about ourselves as being our essence. We narrow our sense of self to the information we gain and use it to foster the growth of the "little" false, autonomous self. I think this is what Jesus had in mind when he counseled his disciples, "Those who find their life will lose it, and those who lose their life for my sake will find it" (Matt 10:39). I think he was telling them (and us) that any time we get lost in the narrow little self, we lose sight of the true Self in God.

How, then, do we avoid this trap of the narrow self while yet opening ourselves to self-knowledge? Saint Isaac of Nineveh suggests that such prayer can expand our hearts: "Be at peace in your own soul....Enter eagerly into the treasure house that is within you, you will see the things that are in heaven for there is but one single entry to them both."[8]

Dogen, Zen master of the thirteenth century, says it is impossible to know the Self without relinquishing the self: "To study the Self is to forget the self; to forget the self is to be enlightened by all beings."[9]

Perhaps what we do is recognize a prayer, a willingness for this knowledge deep within us. We might intentionally pray "God, let me see myself as you see me," or "Teach me about me, God." We might choose a prayer we've read that helps express our willingness. For some, the prayer of Evelyn Underhill is such a prayer: "Jesus, show me what the attachments and cravings are which hold me down below your level of total self-surrender, real love. Show me the things that lumber up my heart, so that it cannot be filled with your life and power."[10]

Some may find a fitness in the prayer of Macrina Wiederkehr: "O God help me to believe the truth about myself no matter how beautiful it is."[11] We might not even name what we are doing as prayer, but there is a humility that prompts us to expose our hearts to the searching light of God's love, embedded in the core of our beings.

However we pray, however we approach self-knowledge, it is important that we detach ourselves from results, that we resist the temptation to make something happen. To do this we may need to move out of traditional methods we've used for coming to know ourselves. Zen meditation might be an appropriate means for this. It is a way of fostering the "diligent awareness" that I spoke of in the introduction. This form of prayer is an act of relinquishment. It is a voluntary letting go of our own agendas, our normal ways of thinking and seeing, thus clearing space for knowing. We might say that it is a death to the "little self" so that the true Self might emerge.

In Zen meditation we sit, usually with a community or at least with a conscious connection to people supporting us. We may plant an intention such as "freedom for love," but we are not there to make that or anything else happen. We are simply disposing ourselves for seeing. Here we learn to watch the thoughts, emotions, bodily impulses, exterior events, all without judging them, identifying with them, or engaging with them. As we come to sit, time after time, watching all these things come and go, we begin to realize that we are not our thought or our emotions or our bodily impulses. We sense a depth beyond the ripples, our true Self that is the sacred source we share with all creation. One person expressed his experience of sitting meditation in this way: "It's as though the eyes of my heart were "Windexed" and I could see things in a new way."[12]

"I Look at God, I look at You"

Julian of Norwich offers a way into prayer similar to Zen meditation in that it "Windexes" away our biases so we can see with God's eyes. When asked by a friend how she prayed for her, Julian responded, "I look at God, I look at you, and I keep on looking at God."[13] The point is that Julian detached herself from her way of seeing her friend and what she wanted for her friend. She turned her eyes beyond her friend, perhaps through her friend, to the God within.

Julian's way of praying for others may be our most effective means of praying for self-knowledge. Perhaps for a time we give up looking at ourselves and keep our eyes focused on God. To look at God is to look at all of creation, seeing the shared God-life of all. As we do this, as we see the bigger picture, we also see ourselves in relation to it. We are freed to see our essential goodness and our desire to live in love, to be love. We also begin to notice our blind spots, the places where we cling to the little self for fear of losing ourselves, the places of attachment that keep us from living who we are. We cannot make ourselves free. We can only pray to live into freedom, seeking God even in the midst of our attachments. In the process we may realize that John of the Cross is right when he says that we come to God through what we love and desire.[14] We may find that our attachments are the vehicles of God's purifying love in our lives. They are the means through which God burns away the impurities of lesser loves until we are but one pure flame. We give ourselves to the fire:

> Learn from the energy of fire. We destroy, we consume, we transform, and in the process we bring health and warmth to life. You are in an era of change when old ways are breaking down. Accept and move with that change in yourselves. Let acquisitiveness or greed or desire for power burn out in you. In their place will arise a clear awareness of the whole. Love and sharing will grow in you as will the creative fire to find the means of expressing them. Fire melts and tempers; let the fire of love do the same with you.[15]

We live in the ashes of our freedom.

4

Help Along the Way

Spiritual direction can be a valuable tool for us as we seek to live discerning lives. For some it becomes almost indispensable. It is an arena for discernment, a time when the words can stop and in the prayerful company of another or others, we can listen. As mentioned in chapter 3, Buddha in his own way pointed to the importance of a kind of spiritual direction when he spoke often of the necessity of being in the company of "admirable friends." It is reported of him that he frequently reminded people that "although one is responsible for treading the path oneself, one can benefit from the wisdom and encouragement of those already familiar with the way."[1]

In this reflection I will be describing spiritual direction from my experience primarily in a Judeo-Christian context. However, I do not mean to imply that this is the only context in which spiritual direction can occur. Any time people desire uncovering the true Self, of divesting themselves of idols, of allowing their deepest aspirations to motivate their lives, spiritual direction can be relevant.

What is needed is the "admirable friend(s)" willing to engage in the compassionate action of listening.

Spiritual Direction and Prayer

The prayerfulness that is the basis of one's ongoing discernment is also the basis of spiritual direction. This prayer begins when a person realizes the desire for spiritual direction and prays to recognize the right spiritual director or group. It continues through the discernment process of the people who are considering coming together in direction. After an exploratory conversation, each prays to know whether or not to begin the direction relationship. These individuals may look for things like a sense of prayerfulness when they are together, or a freedom to accept others as they are without imposing an agenda, or the relative ease at being oneself. (I say "relative ease" because I for one am never very comfortable in initial conversations talking about myself.) Each accepts responsibility to pray for the other, to hold their relationship in prayer, and to talk periodically about whether or not they should continue to meet.

Prayerfulness, then, is part of the contract that people in spiritual direction make with each other and it is the atmosphere of each meeting. It is nourished consciously by beginning and punctuating meetings with prayerful spaces that allow those present to be in prayer together. In the words of the poet Hafiz, the silence supports the people gathered as they "try to listen to what the beloved's eyes most want to say."[2] In the ongoing discernment about the rightness of the spiritual direction relationship, continuing their prayerfulness is a primary consideration. Together they look at their conscious awareness of attending to God as they are present with one another. Hopefully there will be the spillover of this prayerfulness into the rest of their lives.

The prayerfulness of the spiritual direction meeting is more important than the knowledge, skills, and style of those gathered together. Honoring the belief that the Holy Spirit is the real director, the participants meet on a regular basis to allow space for those seeking direction to come in touch with their Center and the direction emanating from that Center. These people must be willing to accept responsibility for ongoing prayer in their lives, whatever that may mean for them. They must be willing to open the various facets of their lives to prayer and also to bring what they see in this prayer to spiritual direction. In the spaciousness of prayer they may better notice the congruence between their participation in life and the direction of the Spirit. Whatever the content of the spiritual direction dialogue—spiritual practices, life experiences, feelings—it should be viewed through the lens of discernment: How does this fit with my overall sense of my relationship with God or with what has been going on between God and me lately? Have I been able to pray about it? Can I pray about it now? Often it is the prayerful atmosphere, rather than any words spoken, that clarifies the vision of the person seeking direction.

If spiritual directors are going to assist in discernment, those who seek direction must be willing to share what is going on in their prayer lives. While this sharing needs to be part of the spiritual direction conversation, especially early on, it must be approached with deep reverence for the mystery of one's relationship with God. Directors may get inklings of this relationship and may even be able to assist others in uncovering the heart of it for themselves, but they can never presume to know the whole of it. We will never know the whole of our own relationship with God, let alone anyone else's.

The Relationship between Images and Experience

As we begin spiritual direction, we need help recognizing that we actually have a relationship with God and then finding language to talk about it. At first we might be inclined to talk mostly about our images of God. We might say to a spiritual director, for example, "I was the youngest in a large family and my oldest brother always watched out for me. It was like he was always around even when I didn't see him. Sometimes he'd give me special little gifts just to let me know he was thinking about me. I realize now that my brother gave me a way to see God." Or, we might derive our image of God from a person who was very critical of us, making us reluctant to do anything for fear of getting it wrong.

Our images of God often outlive their usefulness. Sometimes we hang on to them as a defense against change or the letting go that life often calls us to. Our images of God may or may not reflect our lived experience of God. It is our direct lived experience that we are seeking to explore in spiritual direction.

One way to begin this exploration might be to recall experiences or moments that stand out as exemplifying the way God has been for us. For instance, I am still reenergized as I remember a time of prayer in the midst of great confusion many years ago. Without even knowing what to pray for, I heard in my heart the words, "You shall know the truth and the truth will set you free." Courage and trust were there for me then and come alive even now as I recall the experience.

Another suggestion might be just to let images from nature, scripture, literature, music, and art speak to us about our experiences of God. A person whom I was with in spiritual direction spoke of the experience of watching a tree being pruned and hearing from the gardener that he needed to prune the tree at the places of healthiest growth so the whole tree could flourish. She saw that as a metaphor of God's way of being with her at that time in her life. Another spoke of the work of the Sufi poet Jelalludin Rumi as being especially illuminating. I find for myself and others that it is often something outside our normal range of consideration that most facilitates fresh ways of seeing.

It is also useful to outline the stepping-stones of our spiritual life—the key experiences that seem to have moved us from one place to another, or that indicate that a shift has taken place. We might begin by asking ourselves, "What's going on in my life right now that compels me to consider spiritual direction? What was going on before this? How did I get there? Is there a particular fork in the road I can recall or an event that seemed to change things?" The key in this is to go as far back as we can, noting turning points in our life and what seemed to precipitate them. Once we've done that, we might look to see if there is any similarity in these turning points—for instance, any challenge, invitation, or assurance that they all seem to offer.

I am suggesting a prayerful approach in which we ask God to tell us about God's self-revelation and communication in our lives. This approach can help us uncover the underlying thread of what it seems God has been saying to us all our lives, or what God's prayer in us has been. Through this approach, we might begin to see how we have been drawn to respond to God's prayer in us. We bring these observations to direction early on so that they can become the backdrop for future conversations about discernment. A spiritual director might say, for instance, "Do you remember when you told me that you seem to have been given a deepening trust of the Spirit's work in you? How does what you are experiencing now correspond to that trust?"

Finding One's Authentic Prayer

Inherent in what I have said up to this point is the assumption that we are always able, or at least sometimes able, to access our God relationship. And yet we know that this is not always the case. Some people have never had an image of God, or even strongly felt the presence of God. They've lived their lives in deep faith accompanied by strong doubt. There may have been a time when images of God were relevant for them, or when they could name who God was, but that assurance has been taken from them. In such times, for such people, the spiritual director becomes more an encourager than a clarifier.

Many people will say that they don't know how to pray. They want someone to help them pray, and this often brings them to spiritual direction. The temptation of companions can be to collude with them in bypassing their natural way of prayer in favor of some "right way" to pray. It may take a number of conversations about people's family, work, hobbies, and leisure to help them claim how they have been praying. Sometimes people realize that they have been praying out of old images of God that are no longer relevant for them. Then the question might be, "How would you like to pray?" or "What prayer do you think might fit with what you have told me about the way God and you seem to be together?"

Moving to the Holy Center

Often when people have taken the time for intentional prayer just before coming to a session, they are able to speak with clarity of the spiritual relevance of the material they are bringing, a clarity not readily available to them when they've come without preparation. It is ideal when companions can be present with people as they move through several days of retreat or at least meet with them very soon after retreat. I often see a whole different side of people as they move closer to their holy Center and live in that place of prayer for several days. Often as they resume their busy lives I can remind them of what it was like for them to live in that holy Center. Many times I find that spiritual direction sessions seem more prayerfully focused after times of retreat.

There are other ways in which we come closer to that holy Center during ongoing direction. The silence that ensues after the person has shared something very poignant may become a moment of deep prayer for both of us. The quiet may just happen, or I might ask if the person would like some quiet time to pray over what was just shared. When appropriate, we then talk about what went on in the silence, about what it was like to be with God, or about the person's reluctance to be with God at that time. Occasionally I may ask if the person feels comfortable enough to share her prayer as it is happening. When this can happen without disrupting the prayer, I get a deeper insight into the prayer than if the person merely describes it later on.

Our willingness to be prayerful during direction, to be present in an attitude of discernment, is essential. This is the responsibility of both spiritual directors and those seeking direction. So long as we are clear that we are about God's work, not ours, we will be free to trust the goodness of God for all concerned and to open ourselves to that Presence. Ultimately, the work of discernment is between God and the individual. For a time, we are there together to give ourselves to the *faithful listening* that is meant to characterize all of life.

Evelyn Underhill reminds us, "The creative life of God is always coming, always entering to refresh and enhance our lives."[3] Spiritual direction is one arena in which we can reflect on how we have experienced this creative life of God entering our lives and how we have prayed in response to it. However, spiritual direction itself is also an expression of the creative life of God. In our time together we recognize with the poet, Antonio Machado, that "beyond living and dreaming there is something more important: waking up."[4] In his poem, "The Water Wheel," Rumi tells us that "our friendship is made of staying awake."[5] Together we wake up and stay awake to the newness of life being poured forth in this moment.

5

Choosing
from the Center

As we become aware of our freedom, we sense a depth we have not yet come in touch with, and sometimes we are impatient in the waiting. We repeatedly ask ourselves, "Who am I?" Instead of simple living with the question, we push to answer it. In so doing we get caught in a duality between our being and our doing. We find it easier to allow our doing to define us than to wait in our emptiness for our being to emerge. We know that in reality there is no separation between our doing and our being. We know our compassionate action is, in fact, an expression of our being. We struggle to live in the place of our being, yet we have learned over and over again from our experience that it is only in the faithful *being* that we can see the *doing* clearly. We are reminded of this especially in the Gospel of John. Here the words of Jesus frequently exhort us to abide in him, to live in the place of our true identity. Separated from this place, apart from him, we can do nothing.[1]

That is why, in his *Spiritual Exercises*, Saint Ignatius advises those desirous of making a significant life decision to pray first to know their true identity. Only after months of prayer for this self-knowledge are they encouraged to pray to know how they are being called to participate in God's creative imaging for the world. Their choices become expressions of their being.[2]

From a different tradition, Joko Beck, wise Zen teacher who makes practical applications of Zen for everyday living, says:

> What really decides any problem is the way we think in our hearts. How we see what our life is. Out of that we make our decision....Serious practice changes the way we see our life, and so what we do with that life begins to shift. People want a mechanism for making decisions, for solving problems. There can be no fixed mechanism. But if we know more and more who we are, out of that we will make our decision.[3]

There are times when we simply know, without hesitation, the decision that is ours. Saint Ignatius describes this when he says, "There is a time of clarity which comes with undeviating persistence. We think of the dramatic change in St. Paul on the road to Damascus, for once he began to respond to the Jesus whom he had been persecuting, he never hesitated."[4]

Acts of Discernment

In his book, *Living in the New Consciousness*, Hugo Enomiya-Lassalle speaks of these times of clarity as related to "mystical thinking." He describes this as "thinking that is free from all disorganized limitations, something that is possible only after a long process of purification." He cites Johannes Tauler (great mystic and preacher of the Middle Ages) as saying that "a person who has arrived at this understanding, 'knows in a moment what he should do, where he should ask and what he should preach about.'"[5]

Enomiya-Lassalle suggests that there may come a time when such knowing is more the norm than the exception. I think that happens as discernment becomes a habit, an ongoing way of seeing, of responding to life. Yet most of us are not there yet, or not there yet all the time. And so, for most of us there will be the need for periodic acts of discernment. There will always be a place for our actively and consciously bringing particular decisions to prayer, viewing them through the lens of self-awareness, listening to the Spirit's guidance deep within us. Often, what is most important about the act of discernment is not really the decision itself or the process we use to arrive at it, but rather the process of opening to God through the decision and the learning that takes place in the process.

Acts of discernment have much to teach us about our true identity and about the freedom or lack thereof to live in that identity. The very fact that we may decide to seriously consider a course of action that we have previously not considered may offer some perspective on how parts of our true Self are gradually being uncovered. We may become aware of core values that hadn't shown themselves before, or a direction in which we are subtly being drawn without having noticed it.

Choosing to pray or not pray about a decision, to give or not give ourselves to the Mystery beneath the surface of our knowing and our wanting, can speak to us of our belief in and trust of the reality of that Mystery. It can also tell us something about our need to act as though we were autonomous.

There are other cues we might pick up as we notice how we approach acts of discernment: our striving to "get it right"; our hesitancy to acknowledge our fear that if we open ourselves to Mystery what we discover might not be what we want; the gentle ease with which we consider different possibilities—all of these and others give us insight into ourselves. They may also force us to deal with questions such as: What do I believe about our connectedness with the Divine when I seem to lack the freedom to choose what I sense is most fitting? Am I left on my own until I have gotten "on track" again? Is there only one right choice I can make or are there perhaps numerous right choices? How do I define right choices? Who holds the key to them—God? Me? God and me together? Does God have a certain course of action in mind for me or do I cooperate with God to create possibilities?

Ultimately acts of discernment can invite us into prayer on the meaning of our lives. Thomas Merton suggests this when he writes: "I am a word spoken by God.

Can God speak a word that does not have any meaning? Yet am I sure that the meaning of my life is the meaning God intends for it? Does God impose a meaning on my life from outside, through event, custom, routine, system, law, impact with others in society? Or am I called to create from within, with God, with God's grace, a meaning which reflects God's truth and makes me God's word freely spoken in my personal situation?" Perhaps we will find Thomas Merton's response to his questions ringing true for us: "My true identity lies hidden in God's call to my freedom and my response to God."[6] What is that call? How do I discern my response in this moment?

Some Personal Examples

Reflecting on my own experience has helped me to formulate some scenarios for decision making. Perhaps you will recognize yourself in one or more of them.

While in conversation with a staff person in a program I was directing, I came to suspect that the person was thinking about resigning from the program. I wanted to say, "Think about it long and hard," but that didn't seem appropriate. The person was a real asset to the program, and I couldn't begin to imagine a replacement. I didn't want to think about it.

I'm great at procrastinating, especially when a decision feels weighty and I'm afraid I'll make a mistake. A nervous voice inside begins to chatter, "Oh, don't start thinking about that now. There's plenty of time. Wait awhile. Maybe there won't be any need for a decision. If there is, you can get to work on it in a hurry when you know for sure what you have to decide." I like that rationale. It gives me a good excuse to do what I want to do anyway—avoid the hard thing. So I kept putting off thinking about a new staff person, even when I knew I really did need someone.

When I realized what was happening and was able to invite God into this scenario, what I sensed deep inside was very different from what I heard in the surface chatter. If what I sensed had words, it would have been something like, "Rose Mary, I'm with you in this. You have what it takes for this decision. Gather the information you need. Let it sit in your heart for a while. Do what you can do. Don't hold back in fear. Does it really matter if you make a mistake? What is a mistake, anyway? I'm with you, no matter what."

Grounded in that awareness, I was able to look for someone. In the process of interviewing people I had the assurance that God was as intimately caring of the program as God was of the person who was resigning. I knew that what was good for this person would be good for the program as well.

At another time, in a similar situation, I also found myself not acting. This time, though, my nonaction was not procrastination; it was an act of trust. It felt expansive and open rather than constricted and unyielding. As I prayed about what I should do, I knew that waiting was what I had to do, at least for a while; what I needed to decide would be revealed at the appropriate time. I kept the decision tucked in a prayer for openness and waited until I knew what I needed to do. There was a clarity, a sense of leading, without much effort on my part. I trusted that clarity, although I am still hard-pressed to give cogent reasons for it. I don't always get a clear sense of what's called for in prayer, but clarity can happen sometimes.

At a time when I was considering changing jobs, I didn't have much to go on except that I sensed it was time to begin making a choice. A spiritual director was very helpful for me at this time, inviting me to claim the evidence I had from the past that God had been with me up until then. I knew I had no reason to believe God would leave me to make my decisions alone. I also knew that even though it seemed I wasn't getting much help from God then, everything I had received from God in the past would assist me as I went through the decision process. Reluctantly but trustingly, I began to do what I could. In retrospect, I wonder if God's seeming silence in these circumstances isn't a tacit act of God's trust in me, inviting me to claim what I already know. In the end, I didn't change jobs. But the final decision seemed secondary to what I learned about myself and what is really important to me.

There are times when I move too quickly in settling matters for myself. A superficial voice tells me that I have a responsibility toward other people. The image of myself as a responsible person, with all its "shoulds," kicks in. I pray a little about what I am to do, just to get me started.

I don't hear much because I'm really only talking to myself about what I need to do. Platitudes such as "If eventually, why not now?" and "When there's no wind, row," come to mind. They offer the confirmation I want. I'm off and running, as though it were all mine to do. When I stop to breathe or get my bearings, I sometimes recognize that there is a voice deep inside me wanting to be heard. Often, in moments of grace, I'm willing to listen. What I hear is both invitation and challenge: "Stop working so hard. Be still! Let me do this." If I feel that I've reached the limits of my capabilities in making the decision, I can say very graciously, "Of course." If I have been making giant strides on my own, this yielding is more difficult. I say yes for a little while and then when things don't seem to be moving quickly enough, I try to take them back into my own hands. At times when I don't like what I suspect the outcome will be, I just want to quit for a while. And so I do. Then I'm back to the pushing and the yielding. Life goes on and no one has really been undone by my process, despite the fact that I've taken it all so seriously. God seems to say in many ways, "See, I'm here for all of you."

There are times when I only know by hindsight that I've made any decisions. It just seems as if God and I are together in the process of life. It's hard to tell which of us is doing what, and that's just fine. What's important is that we are together, doing the next thing there is to do. When I look back in times like that, I'm sometimes surprised at where I've been and where I'm going.

As I reflect on the various ways I've made decisions, I am convinced that the final decision itself really is not of prime importance. There are few decisions that are irrevocable. What is important for me is the transformation to which I give myself as I engage in the decision process.

I am learning that there is not a single, universal process for me. For now it seems to involve waiting, trusting that what I need will be given me when I need it. To do other than wait would be unfaithful. Yet there have been times in the past, and I suspect there will be again, when trust shows itself in my willingness to put the gift of all of my faculties at God's disposal, fully using them as I move toward an outcome.

I can't take for granted the process I am to use at a given time. There is a place deep inside me where I am with God. I must return to that place time and time again to sense what is called for in any given moment. Eventually, it won't be a matter of *returning* there. I will *live* there. Then the process I use won't be such a big deal. It will flow from who I am, perhaps taking different forms at different times, but always reflecting who I am in God.

Several of these scenarios blended together in my decision to leave Shalem Institute, a place I had worked for thirty years and dearly loved. In the early stages of that decision process, someone whom I hadn't seen for a while asked me what I liked about working there. It took me less than a second to find a response. I talked about Shalem as being a community of people who are characterized by the very thing that we offer to others: a simple, open presence to God moment by moment. I explained that we didn't always do it that well but that it was important to us. I said, too, that we are a fun-loving, iconoclastic community, unafraid to dismantle our illusions of self-importance.

I also spoke of how Shalem sought to fulfill the mandate of Mother Theresa Gerhardinger, the foundress of my religious community: "Sisters, wherever you are, join the prayer of Jesus that all may be one." I recalled a time during my residency for the Spiritual Guidance Program when a participant said, "All week I've been trying to figure out how we got to be a community so quickly. I finally realized that it's because you get us looking at God first and then at one another." I might describe that a little differently. I might say that people come to the programs because they have been looking at God, or perhaps are beginning to realize that God has been looking at them from within themselves, drawing them through the stuff of their lives into that place of oneness. They are looking for a way of honoring that awareness. When they come to Shalem they find themselves in a community of people all wanting the same thing, although they might use different words or even different theologies to describe what they want. Being able to hang out regularly with people who want to claim what is most important to them nurtures me in my ongoing prayer. Together we experience the oneness for which Jesus prayed.

I spoke of many other things, including how Shalem had nurtured my creativity, until I finally said, "I am so grateful for what I've had all these years at Shalem. Not many people have the opportunity to spend thirty years doing what they most love."

The person with me grew quiet for a while then said, "Rose Mary, I don't get it. If all you say is true, why are you leaving Shalem?" The best I could say to her and to myself was, "It seems like the right thing to do."

Because it seemed right didn't mean there weren't moments of doubt, of uneasiness. In fact, often in moments of greatest satisfaction, out of nowhere would begin this mind bombardment: "How can you give this up? You love it so much and it fits you so well. You don't have a clue about your next job. Where will you ever find anything as good for you as this?"

I didn't have a satisfying answer then. In fact, I still don't have one now. In moments of doubt about this decision or others, I am drawn to remember a time in my life, many years ago, when I was in a similar situation, with an important decision looming. I tried to come at it with all the responsible reasoning I could bring, but to no avail. Having exhausted that process, I finally yielded to prayer—not graciously, you understand, but desperately. Somewhere in the course of that prayer, with my back against the wall, I was given the words from John's Gospel, "You will know the truth and the truth will set you free." With those words came a deep peace and a trust. I didn't "know" any more than I had before, but I could trust that I would know when I needed to know. In moments of doubt, I find it best to surrender myself to trust.

Have I been deluded or mistaken? Have some of my decisions come from some ego-driven place in me that I don't recognize? My life experience tells me that all of these are real possibilities. However, my life experience also tells me that the Spirit abiding within is not dependent upon my purity of intention or unambiguous motives. I can't help but be aware of God's faithfulness for me and through me for others despite my foolishness at times.

Writing to her father about her decision to leave France and come to America with her parents, Simone Weil said: "It seems as though something were telling me to go. As I am perfectly sure that this is not just emotion, I am abandoning myself to it. I hope that this abandonment, even if I am mistaken, will finally bring me to the haven."[7]

I find a consonance with her words. For Weil, the haven was the cross. I would name it love. You may have another name for this haven.

Methods of Decision Making

Especially during times of confusion and doubt, our discernment may benefit from methods that will help us sort through the content of a decision. For example, we might want to be attuned to inner wisdom, but we may need some process to help us come in touch with the lack of freedom that keeps us from recognizing the guidance of inner wisdom. We might need a process that helps us name our fears or uncertainties so we can open these to God. Or we may need to gather all the facts we think we need to know about a decision so that, having considered these facts, we can let go of them in favor of a deeper knowing.

There are other methods that may be helpful:

- List the pros and cons concerning a decision and weigh these in light of their bearing on what is really important to us.

- Imagine talking with a friend who was faced with the same decision and what we might say to him or her about the decision.

- Talk with friends or a spiritual director to sort through the issues related to the decision.

- Imagine what it would be like to have already made the decision and note the feelings that arise, the true peace or lack thereof that is ours as we see ourselves living into the decision.

- Ask ourselves, as we come close to making a decision, "What is a time in my life when I felt most free, most fully myself? How does what I am experiencing now compare to that?"

Methods as a Way into Prayer

It is important to remember that specific methods, although often very appealing, are not always necessary to discernment. In fact, they may militate against it. As I indicated earlier, there is an inner knowing given at times that is not dependent upon anything we can rationally know about a situation. We know that we know, but we can't explain why. I've had this experience myself. You probably have also. We know clearly but not rationally. Then to convince ourselves or someone else that we are being responsible, we put ourselves through the paces of some kind of methodical process.

To subject our inner knowing to methods is like depending on a map of a given locale when one knows the terrain by heart, or relying on a how-to manual for creative expression. Methods can lure us away from a confidence in God and a listening to inner guidance and move us into a false reliance on facts, or on our own or another's ability to figure out a right course of action. At times we are called to wait for inner guidance to reveal itself. Teilhard de Chardin, in *The Making of the Mind*, reminds us, "Above all be patient with the slow work of God."[8] The author of the *Tao Te Ching* asks, "Who can wait quietly while the mud settles? Who can remain still until the moment of right action?"[9]

Whatever the route to a decision, the path must always be prayer. The methods we choose can never be a substitute for prayer. Always, in all circumstances, we must "pray without ceasing" (1 Thess 5:17). We must live receptively in all of life. Our receptivity will take different forms at different times in life, just as the form and content of the prayer of discernment may vary. Sometimes it will mean sitting with God as we ask ourselves: "What do

I want? What do I really want? How does this fit with what I really want?" or "How does it seem God has been leading me in this past year? How does this fit with what has been going on between God and me?"

At other times it may mean consciously seeking God's guidance and then tucking the decision in our hearts, trusting God, through the circumstances of our lives, to reveal the choice in time. On occasion, we may choose specific times of prayer in order to hold ourselves and the decision in God's light, asking God to illuminate the related issues so that we might see more clearly the choice we want to make. Other times, a more active form of prayer may be appropriate, in which we might expose our fear and uncertainty to God or open to God areas of unfreedom, the nonnegotiables of our hearts that get in the way of our striving for what we really want. And sometimes, our prayer might be the prayer of wordless sitting in the fullness of who we are.

During a time of discernment, as at any time, it is most important that our prayer reflect and honor our relationship with God and that it be an honest expression of what we really want. This authentic prayer is an act of trust in God's caring love. It frees us to be present to God just as we are, living in the fullness of who we are although we may never be able to name this. The more habitually we come to live in this space, and the fewer distinctions we notice between those times of conscious decision making and our ongoing prayer of attunement with inner wisdom, the more we live discernment.

6

Discernment within Groups

Whatever we can say of individual discernment we must also say of communal discernment. Ongoing prayer and attention to their shared life in God must be the grounding of those who come together to discern. What they identify as their shared life in God must be articulated so that their decisions can flow from the sense of who they are together in God. A group, like an individual, may feel it is time bound to make a decision, while recognizing that it doesn't have the grounding it needs to do so. This recognition can be the wake-up call that the group needs to seriously nurture its spiritual identity. So the group does the best it can with the decision it faces, trusting God more than it trusts its own inadequacies. At the same time, the group begins to implement practices that will honor its corporate spirituality. And they may even choose a spiritual director to be with them as they give themselves, individually and corporately, to love's transforming process.

Contemplative Dialogue

In my own experience, one of the most challenging but necessary practices within groups engaging in discernment is that of honest dialogue, what I call "contemplative dialogue." It is the foundation for the contemplative dialogue that both facilitates and manifests a group's way of being together.

Contemplative dialogue isn't easy to define, but there are some qualifiers for it that can help us recognize when it is happening. In contemplative dialogue, no word is the last word. Rather, we savor the space between the words, listening for some inner consonance. In contemplative dialogue we can be with God in our differences, allowing those differences not to become a vehicle of separation but a window into the many facets of God's truth. It is in contemplative dialogue that we can begin to sort out what it is we must boldly claim and what we must let go. It is here that we can begin to see the inclusivity of truth.

As individuals, it is a risky thing to enter into contemplative dialogue. We may well be called to change, to relinquish vested interests for the sake of something larger than ourselves. Of course, there is no risk if we are unwilling to be changed, if we already know what the "right" conclusion should be. We simply go through the motions of discernment, putting forth our best arguments, bringing people to our conclusions. If we don't like what's happening, we can always opt out.

It is also a risky thing for a corporate body to allow space for contemplative dialogue. Doing so may open a

Pandora's box of seemingly irreconcilable differences. Gradually, however, members of a group may come to recognize that they share a heritage greater than their differences. Together they name their common desire to listen, to be changed by what they hear, to finally trust God even more than they trust what they want to hold on to.

Sometimes what we want to hold on to is some false identity, some sense of who we think we are or should be together. If we enter the process of discernment with more concern for protecting a false identity, or for reaching a conclusion that we have predecided we should reach, there isn't much room for change, for transformation. Then the group is simply asking God to affirm its delusions. Contemplative dialogue can manifest a group's willingness to allow God to reveal its true identity, to do a new deed among us.

Deepening Authenticity

I have recently been asked to lead a board of directors through a discernment process. Ordinarily I would ask if I might come to one or two board meetings prior to the one I would facilitate so that I could get a sense of what values dictated the board's decisions, what prayer and dialogue undergird its shared life. But that won't be possible because there are no meetings between now and the time we meet.

What I will do instead is try to talk to all the board members individually. I will try to understand what animates the life of the board and what it is they most pay attention to in making decisions. I will stumble around for the right words for each person, but I will want to hear something about how they feel the board honors the direction of the Spirit. I will ask them to tell me about the decisions which in retrospect they might name the most authentic—those decisions that have honored who they are as a board: "What were the ingredients of that decision making? How were those decisions different from those that violated the integrity of the board?" I will also ask them if they feel urgency in making decisions and what needs to happen before they can make a good decision. I will ask them to open themselves to seeing the non-negotiables they bring to decision making.

I'm not sure what kind of process I will design. Much will depend upon the responses I get from individuals. I do know that the process will be spacious. I will be listening intentionally for the inner direction of the Spirit as I move us through the process, and I will encourage others to do that in whatever way is right for them. The process will allow time for people to name their hopes and their concerns and to hold these collectively in silence. It will also allow ample opportunity for people to pray individually and corporately about their decisions and to openly share with each other how they sense the board is being invited to act. It will encourage an atmosphere of freedom that invites a reverence for difference. Ideally, whatever the tangible outcome of the process, the process itself will have served as a vehicle for the deepening authenticity of the group.

This deepening authenticity will begin to show itself as the group achieves communal willingness to engage with God in all of its work. People may begin to recognize places of unwillingness that hamper this process.

Often times this willingness for God can seem riskier in a group setting than when a person is alone in a decision, especially in groups where there has been no real dialogue previously. We may be saying to ourselves, "Well, I trust myself in this process, but I'm not sure I trust others. I'm not sure that they even pray." It could be also that we have such vested interests in what we think the outcome should be, or what we want it to be, that it is hard to be open to other possibilities.

Our willingness for God does not preclude any of these things. It is simply a willingness to trust through all of them, trusting enough to bring all of our preferences, our insecurities, our unfreedoms into our prayer. It involves frequently asking, "God, is there anything we need to relinquish in order to be able to participate in your life for us, for our world?"

As we come to meeting after meeting willing to engage in dialogue, to pray individually and communally for the openheartedness of the group, to share our prayer and our sense of God's presence in our lives as individuals and as a group, we open ourselves to communal transformation. Then perhaps we can pray as a group with the poet Hafiz, "God, what love mischief can 'we' do for the world today?"[1]

Conclusion

I have returned to this writing several times since I completed the first draft. Each time I have been reluctant to let go of it. Each time there have been moments of discomfort, of concern that I haven't said it all or haven't said clearly what is most compatible with my experience about discernment. This time, as I come to yet another revision, the words of my old friend Ray seem spoken to me right in this moment: "Always something new, isn't there, Rose Mary? Always something new." I sense the relevance of his words for this moment and breathe into a yes. This yes frees me to be with what I see for now, knowing that this is not the whole of what I will ever see about discernment. Nor does it need to be. It is what it is for now—and it is enough. This is what I have to offer now. Ten years from now, as prayer and life continue to season me, I will probably see more, see differently. Then, hopefully, as I look back on what I have written now, I will realize it isn't wrong, it is simply incomplete.

So it is with living a discerning life. We may wish that we could have greater clarity, see further down the road. There may even be times when we look back and say, "If I had known then what I know now, I would have chosen differently." Occasionally we may be given a longer view of our lives, but most of us are myopic and the far view is a grace. We finally begin to accept that it is just this moment that we have. The "what next" will be shown us when it is time, when the what-next moment is here. We don't simply endure this moment as we wait for the next; we join the moment in full-hearted participation. Now is the moment we have, and all of life is contained in it. The next moment will unfold from the faithful attentiveness to this moment. But what if there is no next moment? What if this is all there is? Would this be enough? Could we rest in the peace of knowing we have lived life well because we have lived this moment fully? Perhaps a discerning life begins when we can live each moment as though it were our last and make the choices that matter to us now.

People ask me from time to time what process I use for discernment and how I move through times of transition. I tell them that I don't have any real process. I just try to keep my eyes and heart open so I can see and move with what seems called for.

I am, however, able to name some things that supported me through a time of transition and continue to support me. At first I was reluctant to share these things for fear others take them as right for themselves. But I am naïve. Most of us have learned by difficult experience that it doesn't usually work well when we try to take on someone else's path as though it were our own. The path that's right for us, the practices we need, begin to emerge organically out of the context of our lives and our ongoing prayer. What I say of myself may enable you to see more clearly your own manner of discernment.

For me, spaciousness of living has been most important. Once after leaving one job, I took some sabbatical time before I plunged back into employment. That time allowed me to notice the ways I felt when there were no constraints on my choices. It also helped me notice the images of myself that kept me bound in old ways and fearful of new choices. Most importantly, it opened up luxurious time for prayer and the awareness of my desire to live prayerfully, to be awake, moment by moment.

I continue to create opportunities for spaciousness. Right in the midst of what I am doing I find a way to breathe into my soul, to come home to *me*. I'm not always successful at it, but I know it is what I want and I'm beginning to notice more quickly when that spaciousness is missing.

The gift of this spaciousness is bearing fruit. There continues to be a prayer for the freedom for love planted deep in my heart. I keep touching back into that as I go through the day: "Right here, now, freedom for love." Zen sitting has helped keep me more in tune with my true Self in the moment. It becomes a way of reverencing the sacrament of the present moment, seeing what there is to see in the moment and responding. It is a way into "being at home in the muddy water" (of life), of "bowing to life as it is."[1] It is a way of practicing the habit of discernment.

It has been important to me to look for spiritual community and to avail myself of one-to-one spiritual direction. Although these seem to have played a more important role during the actual time of transition, they continue to have relevance. Here I am with the people who pray for me, challenge me, the people to whom I turn when I need to listen to myself. I know these people don't have answers for me, but they can hold me in my faithful seeing. They can remind me to trust the gradual uncovering of the Light within.

For these past few years it has been the people I have companioned as they are actively dying who have taught me most about appreciating the moment and yielding to the mysterious process of grace unfolding within. They are my real encouragers. They give me strong heart. It is in them that I get glimpses of that Light within and am drawn to trust.

Recently, words from Swami Chaitanya Keerti spoke to me freshly of trust. I offer them to you in hopes that they might kindle your trust and your daring as you seek to live as you truly want:

> The last words of Buddha were "Be a light unto yourself. Be a lamp unto yourself." Don't search for light anywhere else; the light is already there, the fire is already there. Just probe a little deeper into your being, enquire. Maybe much ash has gathered around the fire...just probe deep inside, and you will find the spark again. And once you have found a single spark inside you, you will become a flame soon, you will be a

fire—a fire that purifies, a fire that transforms, a fire that gives you a new birth and a new being. Be a lamp unto yourself.[2]

At the beginning of this chapter I mentioned that I had returned to this writing several times since I completed the first draft. As I looked at the times when I felt drawn to revisit this writing, I realized that, then as now, it was very near the feast of Pentecost, which in my Roman Catholic tradition celebrates the presence of that fiery Spirit burning in each of us. As I return to the parts of the Gospel of John often heard at the liturgy of Pentecost, I am reminded once again that we were never promised a game plan for our lives. What we were promised, instead, was the Spirit who would abide in us always, opening up new possibilities moment by moment, being with us as we live into these possibilities. I pray to trust that fiery Spirit, to allow it to do its transforming work within as I seek to relinquish my need for knowing. I pray to live into the growing trust I sense being given me. I know in this I share good company. On the next page is one woman's story. Might it also be ours?

From A Woman's Life

What Mary knew was just
enough for the usual day:
Pull water, flint fire, bake
bread, smile, pray

the dark orations, sleep, wake,
wait. When pain honed a nerve,
when birth or dying clotted
an hour, she leaned to the curve

of living, resilient to fear,
laughter, suffering.
Partings are a little death.
Each one's journey is a thing

wholly without precedent.
She looked at the sky
for compass. None. She, too,
created a road to travel by. [3]

Notes

Introduction

1. Shalem Institute, located in Bethesda, Maryland, is an ecumenical organization dedicated to calling forth a deeper spiritual life in both person and community. For more information, please call 301-897-7334 or visit Shalem's Web site, www.shalem.org.

2. Mary Theresa of Jesus Gerhardinger, *Trust and Dare* (Menomonee Falls, WI: Inland Press, 1985).

3. Jean-Pierre de Caussade, *The Sacrament of the Present Moment* (New York: Harper and Row, 1989); Thomas Kelly, *A Testament of Devotion* (New York: HarperCollins, 1992); Douglas Steere, *Dimensions of Prayer: Cultivating a Relationship with God* (Nashville, TN: Upper Room Books, 1997).

4. Charlotte Joko Beck, *Everyday Zen: Love and Work* (San Francisco: HarperSanFrancisco, 1989); Robert Kennedy, SJ, Roshi, *Zen Gifts to Christians* (New York: Continuum Press, 2000).

5. Janet Jinne Richardson, CSJP, Roshi, is a cofounding teacher of the Zen Community of Baltimore/Clare Sangha.

1. *An Overview of Discernment*

1. For an understanding of classical discernment see: Thomas Green, *Weeds Among the Wheat* (Notre Dame, IN: Ave Maria Press,

1984); William Delaney, "Discernment of Spirits in Ignatius of Loyola and Teresa of Avila," *Review for Religious* 46 (1987); Abraham J. Malherbe and Everett Ferguson, trans., *Gregory of Nyssa: The Life of Moses* (New York/Mahwah, NJ: Paulist Press, 1978); Johnette Putman, OSB, "An Understanding of Discernment," in *Discerning Community Leadership: The Benedictine Tradition* (Conference of American Benedictine Prioresses, 1988. Revised, 1993), 1–3; Jules Toner, SJ, *A Commentary on St Ignatius' Rules for the Discernment of Spirits* (St. Louis, MO: The Institute of Jesuit Sources, 1982); Shalem Institute's Spiritual Guidance Program, see note above for contact information.

2. For one account of discernment in the life of the Buddha, see *The Wings to Awakening: An Anthology from the Pali Cannon*, translated and explained by Thanissaro Bhikkhu (Geoffrey DeGraff) (Barre, MS: Dharma Dana Publications, 1999).

3. Thanissaro Bhikkhu (Geoffrey DeGraff), 30.

4. *St. Ignatius' Own Story: as told to Luis Gonzalez de Camara,* trans. William Young (Chicago, IL: Loyola University Press, 1980), 9–10.

5. George Ganss says of the second prelude of the Contemplatio: "The idea which was common in most of the preludes in the Second Week, 'to love Christ more' now becomes to love God more 'in all things,'—reminiscent of Ignatius's constant concern to 'find God in all things' of ordinary everyday life." See George Ganss, SJ, *The Spiritual Exercises of Saint Ignatius: A Translation and Commentary* (Chicago, IL: Loyola Press, 1992), note 120, 184.

6. David Fleming, SJ, *The Spiritual Exercises of St. Ignatius: A Literal Translation and A Contemporary Reading* (St. Louis, MO: The Institute of Jesuit Sources, 1978), 8.

7. Ibid., 5.

8. Ibid., 3.

9. Ibid., 109.

10. Toner, *A Commentary on St. Ignatius' Rules*, 291–313.

11. Ibid., 94–144.

12. For an accessible interpretation of John of the Cross, read Gerald G. May, MD, *The Dark Night of the Soul* (San Francisco: HarperSanFrancisco, 2004).

13. Kieran Kavanaugh, OCD and Otilio Rodriguez, OCD, trans., *The Collected Works of John of the Cross* (Washington, DC: Institute of Carmelite Studies, 1991), 373, 377–79.

14. Richard Hauser, "Finding God in Daily Life: Ignatian Spirituality's Heart," *Review for Religious* 54 no. 5 (Sept/Oct 1995).

15. For further discussion of the approaches of Teresa and Ignatius to discernment of spirits see William Delaney, SJ, "Discernment of Spirits in Ignatius of Loyola and Teresa of Avila," *Review for Religious* 46, no. 4 (July/August 1987).

16. Evelyn Underhill, "The Authority of Personal Religious Experience," *Theology* 10, no. 55 (January 1925): #8.

17. Jean-Pierre de Caussade, *The Sacrament of the Present Moment* (San Francisco: Harper and Row, 1989), 98.

18. Allison Peers, trans., *Complete Works of St. Teresa* (London: Sheed & Ward, 1978), 239 and 319.

19. Kavanaugh and Rodriguez, *The Collected Works of John of the Cross*, 179–89.

20. Timothy Fry, ed., *The Rule of Saint Benedict in English* (Collegeville, MN: The Liturgical Press, 1982), 15.

21. Thomas Kelly, *A Testament of Devotion* (New York: Harper Collins, 1992), 74.

22. de Caussade, *The Sacrament of the Present Moment*, 72.

2. *Openness to God*

1. Jack Kornfield, *The Art of Forgiveness, Lovingkindness, and Peace* (New York: Bantam Books, 2002), 184.

2. Andrew Wilson, ed., *World Scripture: A Comparative Anthology of Sacred Texts* (New York: Paragon House, 1991), 187.

3. Wilson, *World Scripture*, 382.

4. Thanissaro Bhikkhu (Geoffrey DeGraff), *The Wings to Awakening*, 195.

5. de Caussade, *The Sacrament of the Present Moment*, 72.

6. Kavanaugh and Rodriguez, *The Collected Works of John of the Cross*, 684 and 248.

3. *Freedom for Love*

1. Edmund Colledge, OSA, and James Walsh, SJ, trans., *Julian of Norwich Showings* (New York/Mahwah, NJ: Paulist Press, 1978), 183.

2. Attributed to Pedro Arrupe, Superior general of the Society of Jesus, 1961–84.

3. Kitty McKinsey, "A New Mother Teresa," *Refugees* 2, no. 131 (2003).

4. Cited on Beliefnet Buddhist Wisdom from Ann Bancroft, *Buddha Speaks* (Boston: Shambhala Publications, 2000), with permission from Shambhala Press.

5. Anthony de Mello, *Awareness: The Perils and Opportunities of Reality* (New York: Image Books, 1990), 41.

6. Douglas Steere, ed., *Quaker Spirituality: Selected Writings* (New York/Mahwah, NJ: Paulist Press, 1984), 103.

7. Patricia Mische, "Whole Earth Papers" #16, Global Education Associates, 1982.

8. M. J. Ryan, *A Grateful Heart: Daily Blessings for the Evening Meal from Buddha to the Beatles* (Berkeley, CA: Conari Press, 1991), 44.

9. Hakuun Yasulani, *Flowers Fall: A Commentary on Zen Master Dogen's Genjokoan* (Boston: Shambhala Press, 1996), 102.

10. Evelyn Underhill, *Meditations and Prayers* (London: Longmans, Green and Co., 1949), 8.

11. Ryan, *A Grateful Heart*, 152.

12. Those wishing to learn more about Zen meditation may want to read Kim Boykin's book, *Zen for Christians: A Beginners Guide* (San Francisco: Jossey-Bass, 2003).

13. Margaret Dorgan, DCM, *Guidance in Prayer from Three Women Mystics: Julian of Norwich, Teresa of Avila, Therese of Lisieux* (Kansas City, MO: Credence Cassettes, 1986).

14. For a discussion of the relationship between effort and grace as regards freedom, see Kavanaugh and Rodriguez, *The Collected Works of John of the Cross*, 303.

15. Dorothy Maclean, *To Honor the Earth: Reflections on Living in Harmony with Nature* (San Francisco: HarperSanFrancisco, 1991), 34.

4. *Help Along the Way*

1. Thanissaro Bhikkhu (Geoffrey DeGraff), *The Wings to Awakening*, 29.

2. Daniel Ladinsky, trans., *The Gift: Poems by Hafiz, the Great Sufi Master* (New York: Penguin Books, 1999), 143.

3. John Kirvan, *God Hunger: Discovering the Mystic in All of Us* (Notre Dame, IN: Sorin Books, 1999), 178.

4. Roger Housden, *Ten Poems to Change Your Life* (New York: Harmony Books, 2001), 24.

5. Coleman Barks, trans., with John Moyne, *The Essential Rumi* (San Francisco: HarperSanFrancisco, 1996), 247.

5. *Choosing from the Center*

1. See the Gospel of John, chapter 15 especially.

2. Fleming, *The Spiritual Exercises of St. Ignatius*, 103–18.

3. Beck, *Everyday Zen*, 180–81.

4. Fleming, *The Spiritual Exercises of St. Ignatius*, 107.

5. Hugo Enomiya-Lassalle, *Living in the New Consciousness* (Boston: Shambhala, 1988), 19.

6. Thomas Merton, *Contemplative Prayer* (New York: Herder & Herder, 1969), 84–85.

7. Simone Weil, *Waiting for God* (New York: Harper & Row, 1951), 59.

8. de Chardin, Teilhard, *The Making of the Mind: Letters from a Soldier Priest 1914–1919* (London/New York: Collins, 1965), #57.

9. Gia-Fu Feng and Jane English, trans., *Tao Te Ching* (New York: Vantage Books, 1972), #15.

6. *Discernment within Groups*

1. Daniel Ladinsky, trans., "The Seed Cracked Open," in *The Gift, Poems by Hafiz* (New York: Penguin Press, 1999), 35.

Conclusion

1. Excerpt from the Meal Gatha cited on the flap of the book by Ezra Bayda, *At Home in the Muddy Water* (Boston: Shambhala Publications, 2003).

2. Swami Chartanya Keerti, Osho Rayoga Meditation Center (cited in *India Times* on the Internet).

3. Sr. Maura Eichner, *Hope Is a Blind Bard* (Wheaton, IL: Harold Shaw Publishers, 1989).